ANWES

Orphic

POESIE

BlueRose ONE.com
Stories Matter
NewDelhi • London

BlueRose ONE.com
Stories Matter
New Delhi • London

For permissions requests or inquiries regarding this publication, please contact:

BLUEROSE PUBLISHERS
www.BlueRoseONE.com
info@bluerosepublishers.com
+91 8882 898 898
+4407342408967

ISBN: 978-93-6452-376-9

Cover design: Shivam
Typesetting: Namrata Saini

First Edition: July 2024

Illustrator's introduction

Mannish Rao Jwade's meticulous paintings take viewers on a fantastical journey through imaginary lands filled with strange architecture, metallic beings, and dreamlike scenarios. As a storyteller, Jwade weaves tales from his subconscious, drawing from diverse sources such as childhood tales of kings and modern social crises. Though he admires artists like Bosch and Ganesh Pyne, his work also shows influences from surrealists like Escher and Dali, as well as indigenous Indian metal crafts and sculptures. This blend keeps his art rooted in a modernist style. A graduate of the College of Art in New Delhi, Jwade has received several awards and participated in numerous exhibitions and art projects. Born in 1972, he lives and works in New Delhi, India.

Foreword

The following compilation of poems is a telling of all the tales I wish to share in hopes of finding commonality with many - a time that flew by faster than I could have imagined. In these pages, you will encounter moments of grief and love, the consequences of choices made, the turbulence of relationships, and my own stumbling as a mere teenager along the cobblestones of life.

I have had the honour of working with Manish Rao Jwade, and have used some of his paintings as part of the illustrations of this book. More than an artist, he has been a mentor and guide in my pursuit to expanding my creative liberty beyond writing.

Before you dive into my poetry, I wish to share a few words: the chapters of this book are not direct replicas of the chapters we live through in life. Instead, they are poetic interpretations, woven from personal experiences and emotions. My hope is that these words resonate deeply, offering a sense of presence, belonging, and solace to those who may feel unseen or unheard.

May you find a piece of yourself within these pages.

Warmly,
Anwesa Das

Author's Introduction

Anwesa Das made her debut as an author in 2024 with her first poetry collection, 'Orphic Poesie'. At sixteen years old, she is currently a student at OPG World School in New Delhi, India. Anwesa's journey into poetry began with an earnest passion for creative expression and personal freedom, which sparked her initial compositions. Born in Mumbai and now residing in New Delhi, she has deep family roots in Cuttack, Odisha, exposing her to a diverse array of cultures and languages from a young age. Anwesa's early independence and her unwavering dedication to creativity and writing have propelled her to this stage as an author, choosing poetry as her primary medium to convey thoughts and experiences in a uniquely artistic manner. Beyond writing, Anwesa is also an accomplished pianist, seamlessly blending her creative talents in both music and literature.

Contents

Chapter 1

The words of a daughter

Love, your daughter

A hundred years (we'll meet again)

22nd August 2008

Love, your daughter

Remnants of a forgotten reminisce-
Mother and child at peace of mind;
Unfortunately overlooked in past grievances,
On 22nd of August, 2008.

Although she (sadly) no longer lives,
I feel joy to call her my mother;
Precious seven years spent together -
Let's meet again in dreams, *mama dear*.

Look upon me as midnight strikes -
Someday, we shall reconcile in heaven;
Blissfully asleep in this distant memory -
I ask for your blessings and goodwill, *mama...*

Whilst I'm reminded of the good old days
Where we'd bake and draw and together pray;
Forget not the love I hold for you
(I miss you mama)

Love,
Your daughter

A hundred years
(we'll meet again)

Nine years already? Mama dear
Another Mother's day alone
I write to you in secret love
One I shouldn't hold (I do)

I thought of you last night (I did)
I thought of us in your last days
Tears were shed (I screamed inside)
I yelled at those who misunderstood

Grief can never leave oneself
Though thought often (unspoken)
I hope you found reconciliation -
For Shaanti maa has joined you now

A hundred years (we'll meet again)
I'll wish you Mother's day in heaven
I've begun to heal, mama -
Heal myself to trust your love

I almost cried (I held myself)
I found someone who'd sympathise
(I don't think she knows of you)
The only difference? She lived, you died

Don't you worry, mama dear
I'll be there for all you're not
I hope you know I love you, mama
A hundred years (we'll meet again) ...

Chapter 2

Through eyes of mine,
I look around

Misted morrow

'Fore the creatures come awake

The mingling lives of small town folk

Dead of night

Misted morrow

Misted morrow at crack of dawn
The birth of day marks past begone
Wednesday rises from ancestors' dusk
The wind and fog being nature's musk

Man and critter speak silence's words
The morrow's mist left undisturbed
Hours elapsed as passerby flow
Fallen clouds make their presence known

The fog threatens to slowly encompass
'Fore the eventually fall apart
The mist of morrow paves way to death
The death of a familiar - the fog instead

In knowingness of come another morn'
The warmth of light gives subtle comfort
The birth of day marks bast begone
The misted morrow at crack of dawn

'Fore the creatures come awake

Dusk and dawn are precious gems
The dark of rest and peace embraced
Amidst dim yellows of lone candles
'Fore the creatures come awake

These cannot be sacrificed
Rare few moments left unjudged
Ink flurries the wrinkled page
As I yield to solitude, time and again

Art transitions (quite unstill)
Change my only present constant
Thence I yield to bliss and passion
'Fore the creatures come awake

The mingling lives of small - town folk

A life, twice lived, differs between
The meek and bold, the young and old
A life not lived amongst the rich
Is only seen in winded streets

Lowly houses, bearing trees
So unlike the lonely leaves
Dawn and dusk now come alive
Not so hidden by bricks and stones

The feathered creatures come awake
Awake before the humans do
While little boys with contagious smiles
Gather round together and play

'Twas the walks by the mango tree
Silent moments with the ones next door
They speak, they chirp, they move along -
The mingling lives of small town folk

Luxury gives you worth for money
Winded streets a sense of comfort
The house afar always feels home
Among the mingling small town folk

Dead of night

The blissful burns of morrow end
Giving in to dead of night
The stars and angels welcome us -
Twinkle as they watch upon

The silent words that haunt *(we trust)*
Lullabies of nightingales heard
We rest upon the earth (our mother)
Awaiting to be whisked away

Whisked away to realms of depth
Depth of mind and that of *rest*
We thank the end of godblessed light
Giving in to the *dead of night*

Chapter 3

To love and love, and give and give...

Twin flame

Dear Future Mister Mime

He who never knew of her

A letter of love for you, beloved

My love

Two Beloveds Young

All the words I wish you'd know

My dear

Do you ever wonder, love

Is it love...?

An Apology from me to you

Shall we, darling, reconcile...?

Tales of guilt and joy and us

Secretly misogynist

Twin flame

The lovers' love (reddest of red)
The twin flame found it's soulmate's thread
The stars align (as had been told)
Flames of passion now gone cold

The constellations unite again
Love and lust healed from despair
Time can heal (as had been said)
The twin flame found it's soulmate's thread

Dear Future Mister Mime

Dear Future Mister Mime,
Hope you're doing well today!
I wish to say few words in rhyme
On the morrow, in the may

I hope you treat me well, Sir Mime
I don't believe in half and half
For someday, my words will cline
Though I hope the message is passed

I imagine warmth in yours
In soothing glint of candlelight
I foresee a lasting bond
Borne of love and wholesome might

I seek the day to when we meet
I hope to lock your eyes in mine
In heaps of trust I hold my faith -
With all my love,
Mistress Mime

He who never knew of her

The 'lonesome lady spoke again
(Only to herself, none other)
Of how she came upon the prince
Of whom she knows none about

What a danger life can be
Undoubtedly, so suddenly
Love or fondness (she's unsure)
Too mindful of the tortures passed

She unnoticed the midnight clang
Hidden inside the clock tower
As she thought of he who moved her -
He who never knew of her

Oh! Mind magic - the worst of all
For now she sees hope again
To love and love, and give and give
For he might be worth to try *(again)*

(Now) she remained not - so - lonesome
Imprisoned in fondness of the royal
He who never knew of her
Was one for whom she chose to fall

Is it love? She asked herself
Or only plain foolishness?
Regardless, she was enraptured by
A man of heart and goodwill mind

I shall wait for him, she said
I shall let him heal himself
For he who never knew of her
Was the very one she came to love

A letter of love for you, beloved

In gloomy skies and darkened rooms
Amongst the countenance, us two;
One step nearer to you, beloved -
One step closer than day before

I adore when we speak, beloved -
I see the love you've held for mine;
Though misunderstood by strangers,
I've always loved your lingered stare

I hope we stay as close, my love
Hope we never meet our end;
I commit myself to you, beloved -
I give myself for all we have

My love

You've faded past our distant thread,
You've vanished from the river banks;
Through the creaks your love has bled,
As distant bells of wishes clank.

Ages pass till reconcile,
Intimacy being what I want;
Though the distance burns as fire,
For hours with you all pain is worth.

Oh! How long shall time uncease,
What barriers do I persist to quell;
To meet your eyes with my own, darling,
Beneath twilight, I lay and dwell.

Yet, I dangle by your word,
Your word of honour to return;
Enclosed in care for me you hold,
Aye, I wait for you, my love ...

Two Beloveds Young

Love in youth opposed by most
Unmeasured as their wants unfold
In dread of being enforced apart
The lovers (young) behave outcasts

However young those lovebirds are
However much the time has passed
Both blessed as the other's godsend
The lovers' warmth left no regrets

They seek no haste to observe and flourish
Possessing obstinacy to rebel
For both blessed with the other's soul
The lover's love abandoned remorse

Thus although their fondness opposed
Their heartful polyphony covertly sung
Impaired to their unfolded love
Although the two beloveds young

All the words I wish you'd know

All the words I wish you'd know
Words I fantasise I spoke
Those not easy to confide
Those which need time to be told

All the words I wish to say
Buried deep, not thought again
Words I should not speak so young -
The only words that hold my faith

All the words I wish you'd hear
Words I never voice in fear
Ones to question my depth of love -
The love I hold for you, my dear

All the words you'll someday know
Words with my fondness enclosed
Awaiting when you'll know, darling
Why *those* are the ones I chose

Thence the words I wish you'd know
Are the ones that I hold close
As, before us, time unfolds
There'll be a day, beloved - *you'll know*

My dear

Do not misconstrue, my dear
With my words I mean no harm
Yet I'm guilty of denying
That your words have left me numb

I miss our good old days, my dear
I yearn for when you called me love
Yet I guard you from the crows
If only to stay close, lil' one

I fail to say these words in person
Too distressed of what you'll say
But I hope we stay together, dear
I hope we speak again, someday

Don't misunderstand, my love
Do not be the least of saddened
One day, I hope, you reciprocate
The love I hold for you, my prince

Do you ever wonder, love

Do you ever wonder, love
Wonder 'bout my whereabouts
Do you lay awake at night
Just as I do, all alone

Do you trust me to confide
Your deepest, darkest, hollowed thoughts
Do I charm you as you claim
Or were your words faithless - false

Though I shouldn't dwell in doubt
Your ceaseless silence taunts my trust
Did you ever ponder, hun
Why I've loved you, though I'm hurt..?

Nevertheless, I did not leave
Ignored your restless agony
I know you chose to stay, darling
I know we hold no rues today

Is it love...?

Is it love if you've withdrawn -
Is it when I'm left unseen?
Do I love you all alone,
Or would you still prioritise me...?

Can I call your distance 'care' -
Can I assume you're only held...?
I only long your time, my love
(*I do not wish to ask much else*)

You promised me you'll tell me dear
Promised me of your return...
Yet, of you, I've heard no word -
I now surrender to faith and trust...

Can you blame me? When I ask -
If we still remain the same....
Can you blame me when I cry?
Without you, another day...

I wish to (*someday*) hold your hand -
Wish you'd find me worth your time;
Do I still reserve the right
To be with you... to call me mine?

Yet I wonder... is it love?
Or mere responsibility;
Amidst sadness I survive, but...
Is it love you hold for me?

An apology from me to you

Hope it's not too late, my dear
To say words of apology,
Hope I'm not your cause of gloom
(They only end in misery)

Why the sudden distance, dear
Why the lack of words
I'm not used to being so far -
Not used to being ignored

Im truly *truly* apologetic
If I interfered
I promise you, I understand -
I know you're busy, dear

(*Yet*) there's lack of trust, my love
You seem to have your doubts
Isn't ten months quite enough
For one to love and trust?

I don't have much left in kind
So take my words (with faith I hope)
I've only one last thing to give -
An apology (from me to you)...

Shall we, darling, reconcile?

A foot away, countenance apart -
I feel our distance; *doubts arise;*
Falsehood blinded a crooked life
As unsettled voices lay their claims.

Burning, gruesome, torturous pain -
Shattered remnants of my trust;
Drifted from the wall of love
To distorted temples of *indifference.*

Hope suppressed by chilled silence -
Time shall (not) pave way to death
Among the *joy* and *grief* and *dread* -
Shall we, darling, reconcile?

Tales of guilt and joy and us

Haven't I forgotten, love
Tales of guilt and joy and us?
Haven't I laid eyes on yours
An ancient brown *(with things untold)* ?

I don't intend to compare
The likes of you with other men
Yet I find myself come back
To moments spent with you, alone

I don't choose to fall in love -
My soul decides, my heart trusts
Yes, I can choose to move away
(Although I do, I feel like staying)

Haven't we been through enough
(But you seem to misperceive)
Haven't we lived to tell the tale
Of what was love? *(now none remains)*

(She's right) My unnecessity
To not move on from disloyalty
Shall cease me from forgetting *(I won't)*
Tales of guilt and joy and us

Secretly misogynist

Why are you so hated, dear
Why give them the reason to?
Claimed to love me *(though you didn't)* -
Secretly misogynist

You have knowledge, I have wisdom
Both have power *(both are different)*
I have loved you with my all
I have loved with no remorse

You desire the patriarch's role
You encourage wives' silence
Yet you showed me fair respect
Now I question - were they true?

You chose distance, chose to lie
Yet I've only good to say
I still defend you, when I know
You're secretly misogynist

Chapter 4

As I reach oblivion

Unstill

Stoned

Misunderstood

Long lost childlike embodiment

Ignored

The caring most have lived life worse

A mind whose sins have made me sane

Unread, forced, pathetic beliefs

The 'lone daughter

The forlorn angel

The dread of being oppressed again

The need to punish one's wrongdoings

Tears of torture

Unstill

Solitude's bliss, but also constraint
Disconcert gives rise to doubt
Though joy is contagious
All I feel is cruel stabs

Choice - twice lived - does not improve
Shattered gloom and glum about
She who once preached rare wisdom
Finds herself overwhelmed - *surrendered*

Pain and sadness (*suffocated*)
Eradicated joyous thought
She who once found love and loss
Lies awake at night - *unstill*

Stoned

The 'lone abyss, a shadowed dark -
What was then is now dispart
Words unspoken, left ignored
Crucify her heart and soul

She was happy (*now she's not*)
She was once adored by all
Well acquainted to remorse
Now she choked on tears - *stoned*

Misunderstood

The wise are said to be child at heart
Yet the wisest are most illtreated
The choice she made to live her childhood
Was others' to misunderstand

She had no ill intent, she didn't
She only wished to congratulate
Who are they to call her sensitive
When they misunderstand, themselves

Regardless, she never voiced a word
(She feared a second petty argument)
Perhaps - she must be much too kind
To comfort them (*though hurt herself*)

If only had they not misunderstood
If only (*for once*) they trusted her
Just as childlike as considerate -
She never meant to hurt a soul

She had wisdom (*oh she did*)
She forgave them (*not herself*)
Burying unrest deep within her
To comfort those in need of help

For once, she did not seek out others
Feigning non - existent normalcy
For once, she found it easier to hide
For the one person whom she trusted most

She may be wise... but also human
Misunderstandings what she fears most
Confined in dreaded, suffocated silence
To not (again) be misunderstood

Long lost childlike embodiment

A blank state, the useless mind
Words of wisdom blown to dust
Time (which was once divine)
Not a breeze, but restless gust

Constantly, I lay unstill
Once delusion, now a chore
Toxic compulsion devours till
My *life belongs to me no more*

I utter the words "could've been"
Drowned in guilt; regret; remorse
I dare to say "I should've been"
(Yet) my actions betray the words

Lack of passion accompanies loss
The loss of what was once ignited
Ignorance chases the youthful soul
Through long lost childlike embodiment

Ignored

To care is to commit,
To devote your mind and time;
A choice been made to sell your heart
(*Afterall you aren't worth a dime*)

The sins of goodness clash your soul,
Cursed by regrets of devotion;
Barely surviving bows and arrows -
Your love surpassing existing restrictions.

To care is to give it all away,
To greatly sacrifice;
Although it cuts a severe scar
When you aren't reciprocated in kind.

(Yet) your actions never cease,
Regardless how broken your remnants are;
Although (in solitude) you silently confide,
How it hurts - it tortures - to be left, *ignored.*

The caring most have lived life worse

Brutal silence (sacrifice)
The caring most are pushed away
Why shall I be blamed for her -
For stupid youthful fantasies...?

They who shan't embrace their peace
Are undeserving of my trust
They who pave their way to death
Are left among the unfaithful - 'lone

(Yet) the caring left betrayed
They love too much *(but thought too little)*
I refuse to lay abandoned
By those who'd chosen to commit

Once, then twice - *the hundredth cursed*
I was chosen to suffer most
Accused and victimised of love -
The caring most have lived life *worse*

A mind whose sins have made me sane

The wonders of a stable mind
A mind whose sins have made me sane
Contradictory, is it not
When mistakes became silent wins

The rebels are the ones rejoiced
They who spoke - celebrated
She who stuck *herself* to rules
Found *herself* - unliberated

Yet I find myself again
In the clutches of isolation
Beside the lady of unsound mind
All because of discourage

Discourage to speak again
Speak to those who mind me not
The daughter doubts herself again -
She trusts again, *she failed again*

But she learnt the lesson this time
She thought to keep herself away
(Contradictory, is it not)
A mind whose sins have made me sane

Unread, forced, pathetic beliefs

Hoarse whispers overpower the mind
A broken past comes undone
The daughter tries (yet fails *again*)
To reconcile with all she gave

What is amiss is mutuality
As understanding unexists
Amidst the father's obstinacy
Lies unread, forced, pathetic beliefs

She had tried her best *(she did)*
She kept silent (though in fear)
The father's daughter paved the distance
To preserve her last sanity

She who witnessed banes of burden
She who chose herself (not him)
Has seen the woes of brutality
Amidst the arches of obduracy

Yet the daughter tried again
She spoke again, *she failed again*
Amidst the father's misled words
Lies unread, forced, pathetic beliefs

The 'lone daughter

The sound as though an unseen identity
Engulfing her in unwanted anxiety
The 'lone daughter in a house undone
Imprisoned by accomplishments she must once attain

But, god forbid, not a word escapes
For fear she may be misunderstood
Who cares 'bout the one 'lone daughter
Failing to acquire her many desires

An abandoned book is what this is
Pen and paper unfulfilling
Though the 'lone daughter remains 'lone to herself
It is others for whom she maintains composure

Who shall bother 'bout a wish undone
Who shall reflect on her cause of change
The 'lone daughter continues to silently suffer
(She knows her behaviour is untolerated)

She continues to isolate in solitude
For she is the 'lone daughter after all
There's a reason she's 'lone (and continues to stay so)
Since everyone misjudges vulnerability

Who shall wonder 'bout the lady's mind
Who shall percept on her cause of change
For although the 'lone daughter remains 'lone to herself
It is others for whom she maintains composure

The forlorn angel

The forlorn angel lays disgraced
Innocence devoured long ago
Cursed potential now liberated
Hunted by comrades - all alone

She runs away to solitude's abyss
Frightened of what the future holds
She refuted those who denied her freedom
She'd rather survive all alone

Potential kills - she cruelly learnt
Starved predators thirst for hunger
One way remains to retain control -
Her burning passion hidden within her

She longed for undisturbed anonymity
Although the grief unbearable
The forlorn angel lays disgraced
Her cursed potential a bane to her soul

What need has ambition in cruel a world
What point does her potential see
She owns no choice to what she craves
Prompted to surrender to passerby's needs

Thus the angel lays disgraced
Innocence devoured long ago
Cursed potential now liberated
Hunted by comrades - *all alone*

The dread of being oppressed again

Disconcert gives rise to fear
The dread of being oppressed again
All confidants disappear
Whilst you're caged in devil's lair

Forgotten hope lays dead and burnt
Your erstwhile gashes bleed anew
Through agony is when one learns
The weight of letting sufferings through

Sadly, not a countenance aids
The oppressors surge unfettered
You're forced to kneel forth discontent
Your woes and yowls left unheard

Yet you resume in complete silence
Devastated cries forced to abstain
As disconcert gives to fear -
The dread of being oppressed again

The need to punish own's wrongdoings

The clock ticks, though in silence
So heard when it shouldn't have been
3am - too late, too early
Should I be found, *they'll reprimand*

Unease unearthed, unstillness ensued
What were clouds of bliss - now not
It is constant - the need to *work*
The need to *punish* own's wrongdoings

Not unscathed, not a fool
Yet wisdom fails when needed most
What were once thought innocent words
Now have led to the need to punish

False promises deserve distrust
Past sacrifices lay worthless
Threaten myself (I know I do)
For need to punish own's wrongdoings

I'm not blind - I know I'm hurt
Know the curses stabbed me (hard)
I lay weak, succumbed; I yield to -
The need to punish own's wrongdoings

Tears of torture

Tears of torture mark my bane
My silent cries betray my faith
Screams of fury and shattered souls
My desperate yearns for peace, ignored

How singular can life be
Too used to codependency
The ones to care are ones who don't
Whilst I suffocate in misery's hold

Gone is the princess born too naive
Gone are those worth to confide
I lay awake to undying dread
As joy gives way to grief instead

Pretentious acts of bliss fool none
My guilt and regret come undone
For silent cries betray my faith -
As tears of torture mark my bane

मनीष राव

Chapter 5

All the letters I never sent

The Treasured Saint

One's a friend, another's in love

I ask you, panther

Are you lonely? Are you still...

To the lady of unsound mind

How weak of you (to break a bond)

Unacknowledge

You're too forgiving, Meredith

The last of innocence

Never once

Though we tried (the both of us)

The Treasured Saint

Circumstances unbidden are certainly intriguing
For neither foresaw the leaves unfold
The blind eye fooled amidst a mass
As they recognise an angel - unconstrained

The rarity of it's beauty (platonic I assume)
Those eyes as deep as wells of wisdom
The treasured saint plays the messenger's role
Eradicating barriers of reality and fiction

Time hustles, makes haste, then flourishes by
Soon they become your vambrace to hemlocks
The treasured saint offers immortal comfort
(In affection, thus unveiled, in utter solitude)

One's a friend, another's in love

Glasses of wine (half red, half white)
'Round together in yellow light
Greens of christmas yet to leave
As Black & White is drunk by three

Two amongst the crowd stand out
(One's a friend, another's in love)
Both thankful to have the other
In times when they were thrown apart

(Yet) sounds of laughter are unceased
Though unsure, there's fleeting peace
Amongst the pure and gullible souls -
One's a friend, another's in love

I ask you, panther

What are we, oh he who's masked
I ask you, panther, where we stand
Unstill, uncertain, in between
He who thinks so much like me

You encourage mutuality
He who respects my conditions
I ask you, panther, are we close?
Are we friends (or are we more...?)

Time (together and apart)
Shall speak the words I can't accept
I can only wonder thus
I ask you, panther, what are we?

Are you lonely? Are you still...

Are you lonely? (are you still) ...
On the brink to isolate;
Though we may not be as close
It hurts to see you writhe in pain.

I've always found you sweet and kind
Yet you wish you'd rather die;
Love can hurt (you know it does)
Bloodshot eyes show your turmoil.

I hope we can be close someday
Hope to soothe your endless pain;
With me here, I ask again -
Are you lonely? (are you still) ...

To the lady of unsound mind

What a fool, oh my lady
The lady with the unsound mind
Not friend but folly (now I know)
Now I know your cruelty

What a witch, oh she who's cursed
She who made unreal judgements
She who forced me to confide
To the lady of unsound mind

I feel betrayed, I hate myself
To seek your camaraderie
I am disgusted, humiliated
To bare myself to she who's not

She who's not much spoken to
She who deserves her loneliness
She who made me pity and help
The lady with the unsound mind

I can curse you, I ignore you
Formalities shall suffice
I detest you (*oh I do*)
Hear again, Maleficent

Oh! The times I defended yours -
Defended (though I shouldn't have bothered)
Now Medusa, I say goodbye
To the lady of unsound mind

How weak of you
(to break a bond)

You must let go - that is love
Love I haven't felt for long
One you've chosen to deny
Just for sake of dead end morals

Then you claim the lack of trust
Yet you chose to give back none
How weak of you (to break a bond)
Took three days to feel unloved

I felt guilt - I have a heart
Away from thoughts (quite unlike yours)
Someone full of love as you
Is just as heartless *(what a fool)*

We have parted ways (we have)
I was free from undead burden -
When you chose to give back none;
How weak of you (to break a bond)

Unacknowledge

The dreaded moment - tense and still
The one we vowed to unallow
Friendship isn't worth such gloom
I feel sad (but also not)

I deserve it - I have earned it
Yet I took away your job
Should I be remorseful, darling..
Or should I take pride in my hard work...?

I almost told you, let it slip
Out of curious, innocent thrill
She trusted me again, my love
I couldn't find in me rejection

They might be thoughts, they might be words
I might be overthinking stuff
Perhaps I am the one to blame
To hurt you such in this past month

I write the page again, this year
The one we wrote together last term
Such harmless news brings dilemma
Yet I know - things are different

Things are different from years ago
From lullabies, voyages, secret notes
Things are different - you know they are
Though we choose to unacknowledge

I also know - I have earned it
I have now earned trust - *prestige*
I feel strangely disconnected
From what they or *you* think of me

I won't apologise, love
I only offer condolences
Things are different from how they were
Though we choose to unacknowledge

You're too forgiving, Meredith

Have you chosen to depart
Chosen to leave love, darling
Have I always been so blind
To burden you with selfish being?

I've been a shitty friend, my love
The worst of all that I have known
(But) I do not apologise
Since empty words fulfil no more

I was selfish - *victimising*
I forgot our words of promise
Had your trust for two damn years
Under borderline toxicity

I neglected, I ignored
My soulmate in her times of darkness
I've been a shitty friend, my love
Hurt you more than *she* ever did

I once took pride in our close bond
Once thought myself to be kind
Yet (in hindsight) now I see
What a useless friend I've been

You only needed me to listen
Only needed someone's presence
Yet I'm too incapable
To give you neither love nor patience

Do I regret? *Yes I do*
Do I forgive myself? *I don't*
You're too forgiving, Meredith
I do not deserve such angel queens

I miss *us* (you miss *us* too)
Miss the times I listened to you
I miss you speak my name with love
Meredith Charlotte Robinson

Do I long for you? *I do*
Do I punish myself? *I do*
Despite angst, you chose to stay -
You're too forgiving, Meredith

The last of innocence

For once, I come to question us
Question what became of us
Do I alone feel us afar
Further than they let us part...?

We used to be the squirrel and squail
Close as souls ("What a tale!" they'd say)
I miss our days of 'two to tango'
Most of what we had - *replaced*

Can we be close again, my love
Can we revert to what we were...?
'Fore the claws of adulthood claim
The last of innocence (unastray)

Never once

Though I've witnessed growing distance
Never once I thought of ours
I'm unsure of where we stand
As adulthood comes nearer

Oh, how I wished for change
But *never once* between us two
All had left - we chose to stay
(Although we try, we're still astray)

I still remember our very firsts
Our talks and games - all that was worth
We spoke for hours on the phone
(Now? Barely once a month...)

However, I'm not heartless, love
I love you and would never leave
For I know you have none other
To stand beside you when in need

Perhaps these might be tests from God
Questioning our growth apart
But can you blame me, when I say -
"Times have changed - *our minds have changed...*"

Man, I miss the good old days
Though they hurt, we chose to stay
Amidst the blur (just so you know)
Never once I said I'd leave

We have promises to uphold
We have tales to tell the world
For though we witness growth apart
Never once I thought of ours

Though we tried (the both of us)

I'm not angry, only sad
Of ingratitude and depreciation
Why the distance amongst us all
Although we tried (the both of us)

I only wished your happiness
I wished to give back all your love
Surely there are remnants that
I could be proud of growing up

I make mistakes, I learn from them
Though I notice impatience
Times have changed, you know they have
Although you choose to unaccept

I speak for me, I speak for him
I have no courage to confront
The fragile bond amongst us all
Although we tried *(the both of us)*

Chapter 6

For the love of life, I owe these words

To grief and grace and love

Newfound love

Those who only see their own

To those who seek the prodigious

Not all women

Those with morals

The winded path of cobblestone

To grief and grace and love

It's a choice to choose to heal
To grow apart from the uncommitted
I'm not lonely, I'm unstill
(Only 'round the likes of twits)

I wish to be the crystal water
Who slips through fingers but holds the ship
Yet I was burnt to endless ashes
Kindness' forest burnt alive

I have learnt from those around me
To give and give (not expect from most)
Solitude (undeniably)
Gave way *to grief and grace and love*

New-found love

The mind is odd (so's the world)
So's the growth of amateurs
An era (unbeknownst before)
Of clarity and newfound love

"Love of what?" she would've asked
"Fond of one, or fond of all?"
"No idea," I would've said
"New-found love's unpredictable."

Love of stillness, love of work
Love of only three confiders
I have now learnt to adore
Where I was and where I'm now

"This is new-found love," I say,
"Ambitious at a steady pace."
"A love that taught," a wise man said,
'One to be as wise as him.'

I have bathed, cleansed and drowned -
Surrendered to the art of passion
"What was that?" little me would've asked
"New-found love, my darling," I'd say

Those who only see their own

There's distrust, controverse
They who mingle unafraid
Understood not (truth and love)
Once in vicinity, move away

Yet they still have goodness left
Thus they fool the common man
They who call themselves 'your *friend*'
Are truly useless hindrances

Make you question your own worth
Make you doubt yourself *(do not)*
I have chosen to depart
From those who only see their own

To those who seek the prodigious

Equivalence unexists between
Sketchy tales yet to be told
Words (incomplete they are)
Make us kneel before the Great

Yet the Great aren't so
Not all born with unduly good
Some shed tears in dark and gloom
To maintain allegories of perfectionism

Who are we to stand unfavoured
By those who seek the prodigious
Who are we with unbent silence
(Negligence isn't thine to take)

You may take it, ye may leave it
(Yet I hope these words are read)
For all the men and all the mistress
Do not give in to idealist allures

We are none to stand ignored
(For disregard isn't thine to take)
I break my silence (thus I say)
To those who seek the prodigious

Not all women

Not all women are cared and loved,
Not all see the need to hide;
Some are bold and dare to speak -
Speak against conservative cries.

Not all women are household wives,
Not all marry, forced to bow;
Some have courage to preserve
The remainder of their youth and life.

Not all women are restrained,
Not all care for superstitions;
The only ones to remain sane
Are sadly claimed as untraditional.

Not all women are religious,
Not all stand to be disgraced;
Some do not allow themselves
To fall for society's low intent.

Not all women are weak in mind,
Not all scared to break their quiet;
The only woman we should commend
Is one who chooses to unblind.

Those with morals

Humans are blind - utter cowards
They fake their lack through self - esteem
Those 'inferior' are suppressed
Kept in dark - manipulated

Those with morals beg to bow
Beg the world to humble them
Those with morals are unafraid
To learn and seek and bind their fate

They rule the world (they think they do)
Above those much more wiser
They who surrendered to their fears
Forever lost enlightened wisdom

Those with morals forgo age
Forgo the need to reciprocate
They who know the truth of art
Know it's value (unlike *them*)

So the moral beg to bow
Beg the world to humble them
Thence the moral are unafraid
To learn and seek and bind their fate

The winded path of cobblestone

The winded path of cobblestone
Down the arches of treachery
A single road (although undone)
Will lead you past your misery

You can't avoid the devil's lair
A useless call (you must beware)
The winded path of cobblestone
Spares no mercy to weaklings' souls

(Yet) once the treacherous torture ends
The undone road 'comes done again
Once the pain has sought you growth
The angels spare you from despair

Why hide from inevitable hurt
Why be another weakling soul
Someday, unwanted sadness ends -
The winded path of cobblestone

9 789364 523769